Two in the Wilderness

Adventures of a Mother and Daughter
in the Adirondack Mountains

Sandra Weber
Photographs by Carl E. Heilman II

Calkins Creek Books
Boyds Mills Press

*I*f a child is to keep alive his inborn sense of wonder . . . he needs the companionship of at least one adult who can share it, rediscovering with him the joy, excitement and mystery of the world we live in.

— Rachel Carson, environmentalist and writer, *The Sense of Wonder*, 1965

Dedication

To my daughter Marcy who hiked and camped in the woods with me, and shared her journal, poems, and dreams

Acknowledgments

In memory of Grace Hudowalski (1906–2004) and Warder Cadbury (1925–2004)

Special thanks to three experts on the Adirondacks who read the book and offered important advice: Warder Cadbury of Albany and Indian Lake, New York (author, historian, and retired State University of New York professor), Neal Burdick of Canton, New York (author, editor, and Associate Director of University Communications at St. Lawrence University), and Peggy Lynn of Red Creek, New York (folksinger, songwriter, and nature educator).

My thanks also go to my editor, Carolyn P. Yoder, for her expert knowledge and superb skills.

Picture Credits

All photographs by Carl E. Heilman II except for the following: Jacket flap (bottom), Doug Arnold; Page 4, Mapping Specialists LTD.; Pages 16 (top) and 26, courtesy of the Adirondack Museum; Page 16 (bottom), courtesy of the New York State Archives; Pages 21, 22, 28 (left), 30, 37, and 38 (inset), from the collection of Sandra Weber.

Text copyright © 2005 by Sandra Weber
Photographs copyright © 2005 by Carl E. Heilman II
All rights reserved

Published by Calkins Creek Books
Calkins Creek Books/Boyds Mills Press, Inc.
A Highlights Company
815 Church Street
Honesdale, Pennsylvania 18431
Printed in China

Library of Congress Cataloging-in-Publication Data
Weber, Sandra, 1961–
    Two in the wilderness : adventures of a mother and daughter in the Adirondack Mountains / by Sandra Weber ; illustrated with color photos by Carl E. Heilman II.—1st ed.
        p. cm.
    ISBN 1-59078-182-1 (alk. paper)
    1. Natural history—New York (State)—Adirondack Mountains—Juvenile literature. 2. Adirondack Moutains (N.Y.)—Juvenile literature. 3. Weber, Sandra, 1961—Juvenile literature. 4. Weber, Marcy—Juvenile literature. I. Heilman, Carl, 1954– ill. II. Title.

    QH105.N4W43 2005
    508.747'5—dc22
    2004029065

First edition, 2005

Visit our Web site at www.boydsmillspress.com

10 9 8 7 6 5 4 3 2 1

Contents

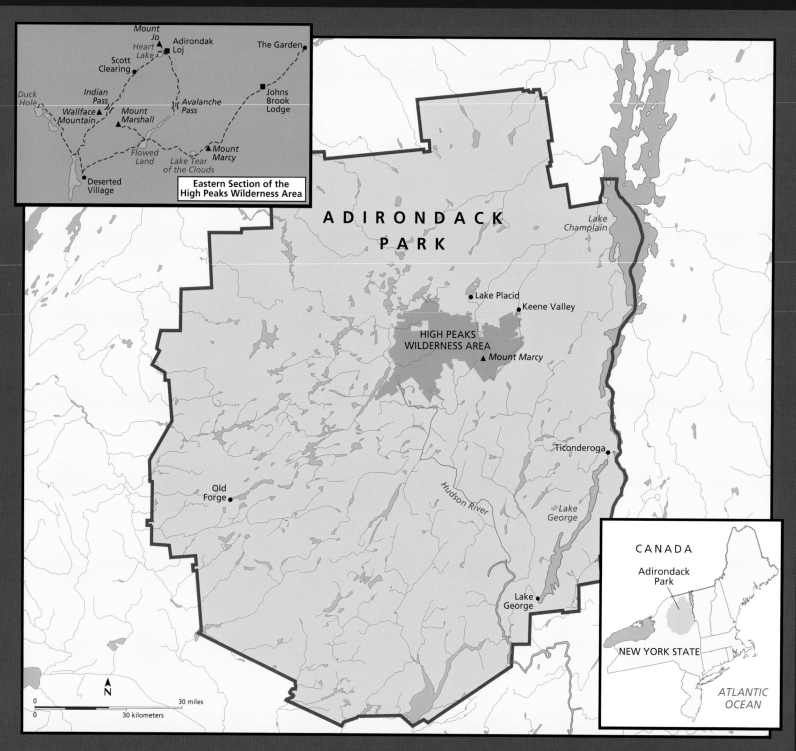

Eastern Section of the High Peaks Wilderness Area

Mount Jo
Heart Lake
Adirondak Loj
Scott Clearing
The Garden
Indian Pass
Avalanche Pass
Johns Brook Lodge
Duck Hole
Wallface Mountain
Mount Marshall
Deserted Village
Flowed Land
Lake Tear of the Clouds
Mount Marcy

ADIRONDACK PARK

Lake Champlain

Lake Placid
Keene Valley

HIGH PEAKS WILDERNESS AREA

▲ Mount Marcy

Ticonderoga

Old Forge

Hudson River

Lake George

Lake George

N

0   30 miles
0   30 kilometers

CANADA

Adirondack Park

NEW YORK STATE

ATLANTIC OCEAN

The Adirondack Park was created in 1892. The boundary was drawn with a blue line and enclosed 2.8 million acres. The "blue line" has been expanded several times. The Park now has more than 6 million acres, almost half of which is public forest preserve. It is the largest group of wild public lands in the eastern United States.

The ADIRONDACK PARK

"The Adirondack wilderness may be considered the wonder and glory of New York."

— Verplanck Colvin, land surveyor
and promoter of creating a public forest park, 1873

THE ADIRONDACK PARK IS ONE OF AMERICA'S GREAT NATURAL PARKS. IT IS A massive area of forests, mountains, and waterways covering the northern part of New York State. It has more than 6 million acres, making it the largest park in the country outside Alaska. It is more than twice the size of Yellowstone National Park.

This is a special kind of park because it contains a mixture of state-owned and privately owned land. Lush forests, quiet waterways, and craggy mountains dwell right beside farms, homes, schools, stores, churches, and factories. About 130,000 people live and work in the Adirondack Park, while millions more come to visit every year. Lake Placid and Lake George are two popular Adirondack vacation spots.

The mountains of this region are survivors of an ancient geological dome of rock that rose up from deep in the earth. It is estimated to be 1.2 billion years old. More recently, in the past million years, mammoth ice sheets swept over the area at least three times. They gouged valleys, reshaped mountain peaks, and created lakes and ponds.

Native Americans began coming in the summers to hunt and fish. People of the Iroquois nations came from the south, and their enemies, the Algonquin people of the Huron nations, came down from the north. Moose, deer, bear, and beaver were plentiful. Beaver pelts were in great demand for making into fashionable hats for European gentlemen. This gave the region its first name, Couchsachrage, which may mean "Indian Beaver Hunting Country."

Some maps labeled the region "Dismal Wilderness" because of the many swamps, drowned lands, and mountains. Other maps simply showed a vast blank space across northern New York.

French explorers visited the region in the 1600s but had no interest in the wild

▲ *Mount Marcy (on the left), 5,344 feet. The Adirondack Mountains are not tall compared with the Alps or the Rockies, which tower higher than 14,000 feet. The Adirondacks are the tallest mountains in New York State, with Mount Marcy rising more than a mile high.*

"I have traveled in foreign lands; have been twice to the Amazon Valley; and I rise to remark that there is but one Adirondack Wilderness on the face of the earth."

— Nessmuk (pen name of George Washington Sears), June 9, 1880

▲ *Entering the High Peaks Wilderness Area. Hikers sign a logbook as they enter the High Peaks. It helps rangers find lost hikers, and it tracks how many people are using the area.*

mountain areas. There was not much to attract settlers, either; most of them passed through and kept heading west. It was the early 1800s before a number of them stayed and built mills and started farming in the valleys.

Scientists began exploring the region, too, and soon a name was proposed. In 1838, geologist Ebenezer Emmons suggested calling the range of mountains the Adirondacks, from an Indian word probably meaning "those who eat bark." This was a name used by the Iroquois to refer to the Algonquins' habit of eating roots, twigs, buds, and even bark sometimes. Soon "Adirondack" was being used to refer to the entire region.

By the middle of the nineteenth century, there were more people and more industries. New hotels opened to house tourists from the cities. Explorers found iron ore in the mountains, and mining operations sprang up. Lumber companies began cutting the pine, hemlock, and other woods. In some places, mountains were stripped bare, and loose soil spilled into streams. Soon, concern grew about the logging and the effect it was having on the water supply. In 1885, the people of New York made a decision to preserve the Adirondack forest before it was too late. They created the Adirondack Forest Preserve.

In 1894, they voted to amend the state constitution to include the "Forever Wild" clause. It says: "The lands of the state . . . shall be forever kept as wild forest lands. They shall not be leased, sold or exchanged, . . . nor shall the timber thereon be sold, removed or destroyed." This was an amazing document because it not only stopped the cutting of live trees but also prevented the removal of dead wood.

Today, many areas once farmed, mined, logged, or burned have generated thick new forests. Wildlife such as moose, eagles, and peregrine falcons, whose populations were wiped out in this region, have returned. A big portion of the

◀ *Crossing a log bridge along the Indian Pass trail. Drizzling rain and heavy backpacks can make walking tricky.*

park, about 1 million acres, has been designated as "wilderness areas." These areas have the strongest protection; almost nothing there is made by man. Hiking trails are permitted, as are a few simple structures, such as lean-tos, outhouses, and ladders. However, houses, roads, and motorized vehicles are forbidden. Even campfires are not allowed in some places. The landscape is being allowed to return to its natural state.

The High Peaks Wilderness Area in the north-central part of the park is one of the largest stretches of wilderness in the eastern United States. It holds Lake Tear of the Clouds (the highest source of the mighty Hudson River) and Mount Marcy (the highest point in New York). It is home to loons and falcons, balsam and dwarf birch, black bear and black flies.

The High Peaks is a place where humans are only visitors.

DID YOU KNOW?

It is difficult to say exactly what wilderness means. To some, it is all outdoors. To others, it is only those places where there is nothing of man's creation.

New York State uses the definition from the United States Wilderness Act of 1964. It defines wilderness as "an area where the earth and its community of life are untrammeled by man, where man himself is a visitor who does not remain."

Introduction

▲ *Above: Pink Lady-Slipper*

▶ *Opposite: Straddling a log across the trail. Hiking poles and stretchy knee braces help keep my legs from getting tired.*

YOU CAN'T REALLY GET A FEEL FOR THE ADIRONDACKS FROM A MAP. IT IS A BIG PLACE with lots of crannies and crevices. Even from an airplane, you can't grasp the calm hush and deep slush of this place. You have to put on a pair of boots and walk up and down and back and forth across its turf.

I have hiked and camped among the Adirondack Mountains for twenty years. I especially love to go to the High Peaks area because it gives me a feeling of wildness. I see great blue herons and pink lady-slippers. I hear woodpeckers knocking at dead tree trunks. I smell sweet balsam, and when I grab a tree to pull me along the trail, gummy sap sticks to my fingers.

My imagination flies free. It feels as though no one has ever walked the path I walk or sniffed the lily I smell. Life is fresh and simple. Mountain springs are my faucet, and wild blueberries are my fruits. A lean-to or tent serves as my bed.

After a few days in the High Peaks, I feel the slow rhythms of nature beating through my bones.

I have always wanted to share this place with my daughter Marcy. When she grew into size 8 boots, I decided it was time for our first mother-daughter backpacking trip. She seemed strong enough to carry a full pack. And I thought that at age eleven, she was tough enough to endure whatever hardships might come our way.

But now worries creep into my brain. I have never camped alone with Marcy; her father and older sister were always with us. I have never been solely responsible for cooking, first aid, and gear. I am afraid bears will get our food. I worry about finding my way through the woods. Can I start the stove? Will my motherly concerns cause fights?

I hope that day by day, the disagreements and doubts and worries will melt away. Somewhere in my head is a teeny-tiny notion that this trip might build a magical bond between us. Maybe the Adirondacks will prove to be a place where Marcy and I can be just two girls in the woods.

Marcy's Journal
Tuesday, July 29

My name is Marcy, and I am eleven years old. This is my journal for a hiking trip I am taking with my mother. We will walk 60 or 70 miles and be gone for almost two weeks. I know I will miss my friends and my cats.

Mom really wants me to go on this trip. She thinks it will be fun. I think this trip is going to be annoying and boring.

Seeing Green

Day 1, Wednesday, July 30

IN THE EARLY MORNING, MARCY AND I TAKE A SHORT scramble up our favorite little peak, Mount Jo. It is hot and sunny, a great day to start a hiking trip.

From our perch at 2,876 feet above sea level, we have a bird's-eye view of the Adirondacks. The soft, pea-green leaves of birch, maple, and beech cover the valley. Higher on the mountain slopes, the deciduous trees completely disappear, and dark green balsam and spruce spread their canopy.

In the center of the vast greenness is mountain peak piled upon mountain peak. Some are stripped bare to their rock core. They look so steep and slick that it seems impossible to climb them. But the thought of standing on top of those huge peaks is exciting.

Crossing this land could be challenging, maybe even dangerous. It also looks like fun. Few people, and even fewer kids, get to experience wilderness such as this. We are actually going to live for twelve days in this place once known as the "Dismal Wilderness."

As we descend Mount Jo, we leave the marked trail and push through the trees. In the Adirondacks, this is called a "bushwhack." It means you are hiking off the trail and elbowing your way through tree branches, underbrush, and bushes. Bushwhacking is tough going and you get plenty of scratches, but it leads you to places that are unexplored.

We discover a rocky ledge topped with blueberry bushes. I gobble a few of the sweet berries and then sit down to enjoy the view. Meanwhile, Marcy crawls through the bushes. She is on a hunt for the biggest, juiciest berry in the patch.

On another ledge, Marcy finds a dead animal. She examines its skeleton and the furry remains of its long tail. "A weasel," she says. "Hmm. Maybe this trip isn't going to be boring."

▲ *Above: On the trail to Mount Jo. A short drive from Lake Placid, the little peak offers fabulous views of the High Peaks Wilderness Area.*

◀ *Opposite: Along the trail, Marcy explores the cliffs above Heart Lake. In a few days we will climb the white strip in the distance — a landslide on Mount Colden.*

11

Preparing for the trip. This barrel-shaped canister will protect our food as well as our trash from bears.

Back at the parking lot, I fill my pack with the gear we need for four nights of camping. Every piece of gear must be absolutely necessary, because it adds weight to the pack. We try to bring things that can serve multiple purposes. For example, we are bringing three cups but no plates or bowls; we will eat every meal from a cup. Bandannas are another good item; they serve as sweat rag or nose tissue and then can be rinsed and used as hat, scarf, potholder, or dishcloth.

One of the most important items I am bringing is a big black barrel. It holds all of our food and is supposed to keep it safe from animals. If chipmunks or bears get into our food, the trip will have to end. All of our plans will be ruined, and I will feel terribly sad and disappointed. I don't want anything to spoil this trip.

I try to hoist my 50-pound pack onto my back. Marcy has to help me. I wonder how I will be able to carry this pack if I can't even lift it. But I will find a way.

Marcy carries a backpack filled with her sleeping bag, clothes, and first-aid supplies. Her sleeping pad and tent poles are lashed on top, and a steel cup and a pair of sandals hang from the back. She looks like a real mountaineer.

Photographer Carl E. Heilman II snaps his camera as Marcy and I help each other adjust our packs. He will be joining us at spots along the way to take photos. He likes to hike and camp in the Adirondacks, too, so I know we will enjoy his company. But he will be going back to his warm and cozy house every day; we will not.

Neither Marcy nor I really know what twelve days in the woods will be like, but we are eager to begin. So we say farewell to soap, sofas, and milkshakes (and Carl) and start walking.

Marcy sets out ahead of me on the well-worn trail around Heart Lake and south toward Indian Pass. We will take it easy today and go less than 3 miles.

This forest seems as if it has been growing here for ten thousand years. Actually it is only one hundred years old. A big fire burned this area in 1903, and the forest is still in the process of recovering.

Picking wild blueberries on a sunny ledge

The birch trees that grew in the burned spaces are now old and dying. Balsam and spruce are moving in and will soon return this forest to its old appearance.

By late afternoon, we are pitching our tent beside Indian Pass Brook. Marcy assembles the long poles while I push the tent stakes into the soft dirt. Together, we feed the poles through the tent sleeves and raise the roof. There is just enough room inside for two.

I start our little one-burner gas stove and heat some ravioli and baked beans. It's not fancy food, but it smells delicious.

Marcy takes charge of getting water. She pumps it through a filter because the brook water is not safe to drink untreated. It might contain harmful bacteria that would make us terribly ill.

Surprisingly, Marcy has no trouble with the pump. And I have no problem with the stove. I guess we are both realizing we are fast learners and we make a good team.

After dinner, I sit in the tent and listen to the mosquitoes buzz around the screening. I cannot sleep in the strange surroundings. I also worry about the steep trail that lies ahead, and about the impending rainy days. We are warm and snug tonight, but what about the next week? Rain is predicted for every day.

▶ *Filtering water. Marcy soaks her feet as she pumps water from the stream through a filter and into a water bottle.*

Marcy's Journal
Wednesday, July 30

I suppose this trip is not as boring as I thought. First, Carl Heilman, our photographer, is a fun guy. He bushwhacked over rocks and climbed along high ledges with us. Also, sometimes he makes us walk in slow motion. Other times, he pops up in front of me and takes a picture without warning.

The other excitement today was that I burned my hand. Yeah, the baked beans tipped off the stove, and I dived for the pot. Mom stuck my hand in the cold brook. Then she bandaged it and it felt better.

Concerning our camp: The lean-to was full. So we put our tent in a large, grassy clearing. It is close to the brook and waterfall (Rocky Falls). The gurgling water is very loud.

INDIAN PASS

Day 2, Thursday, July 31

ACCORDING TO LEGEND, AN INDIAN BRAVE HID GOLD IN A CAVE HALFWAY UP THE WALLS of Indian Pass. The entrance to the cave can be spotted only . . .

If moonlight is bright
On the eighth of September,
At twelve in the night . . .

— Henry Van Hoevenberg, hiker, innkeeper,
and storyteller, "The Legend of Indian Pass," 1878

▲ *Above: Blue Gentians*

◀ *Opposite: Huge boulders block the trail through Indian Pass*

As luck would have it, we are here on July 31 and during the daylight. Most likely, we would not climb the cliff anyway. It is called Wallface, and it is 1,000 feet high, straight up. Besides, I do not want to carry heavy gold in my pack.

The morning is warm, the sky completely blue. After a breakfast of instant oatmeal, we putter in the brook. I spot a crayfish wriggling in the shallows. Marcy hurries over to see the little lobsterlike creature. She reaches into the water to touch it, but it scoots under a rock.

Soon we pack our gear and head deeper into Indian Pass. The walking is easy because the trail is wide and flat. This is an old footpath, used as a shortcut through the High Peaks region. The pass cuts a northeast-southwest track right between the mountains.

A very important trip was made here in 1826. David Henderson, a businessman with a sense of adventure, said the excitement began when a "strapping young Indian" displayed a nugget of iron ore. The Indian offered, "You want see 'em ore — me know 'em bed, all same."

Although Henderson thought he might be led on a wild goose chase, he wanted to see that bed of iron ore. He knew what great wealth could be made from iron. So

Right: The Choppers *by Seneca Ray Stoddard, about 1898. During the winter months, lumberjacks used axes and saws to fell trees.*

Below: An old logging dam. In the spring, dams were released and the water carried the logs downstream to a lumber mill.

DID YOU KNOW?

Logging has been an important activity in the Adirondack forest. By 1850, the Adirondacks had made New York the leading producer of sawlogs (large logs that can be sawed into boards). In 1912, the state led the nation in production of pulpwood (logs used to make paper).

Some areas were clear-cut, meaning all the trees were removed and the forest was drastically changed. Other areas were logged in such a way that there was little change to the forest. Axes and saws never touched about 200,000 acres, an area the size of Shenandoah National Park in Virginia.

he asked the honest-looking Indian how much he wanted for taking him to the ore bed. "Dollar, half, and 'bacco," he replied.

Henderson paid the $1.50 and tobacco. True to his word, the Indian led Henderson south through Indian Pass to chunks of iron, "some as large as a pumpkin." Then they came to the ore bed — it was 50 feet wide! Henderson had never seen anything like it. "Here is the great mother vein of iron," he exclaimed.

Over the next few years, Henderson and his business partners spent a great deal of money to mine and process this iron. The investment paid off. The ore was found to be of such high quality that it was fit for making steel. As a result, iron from the Adirondack woods found its way into the first steel ever manufactured in America.

We will visit these old ironworks tomorrow, but right now we have reached Scott Clearing. A man named Scott cut trees and started farming here in the early 1800s. Later, a lumber camp was built in the clearing. We can still see the remains of rusty machinery and metal buckets.

Marcy climbs on top of a 4-foot stone wall. She is fascinated by this man-made structure sitting out here in the middle of the woods. It should be surrounding a flower garden or graveyard, not snaking through a hiking trail.

The wall is another relic left by loggers, part of a dam that was used to hold back the brook water. During the winter, the lumberjacks chopped and sawed trees and hauled the logs to the clearing. They piled the logs above the dam and waited for spring, when melting snow and heavy rains made a pond. When the dam was released, the rush of water floated the logs down the brook to a river and farther on to a lumber mill.

The log dam is broken now, and the pond is gone. All that remains is a marsh, filled with blue gentians. It is pleasant walking through the flat grassland and snacking on red raspberries.

Past the marsh, the terrain changes drastically. The trail becomes steep and climbs over and around boulders, some as big as houses. A jumble of wet moss and tree roots completes the wild mess.

We slip and trip and get our first hint of the difficulty of carrying big packs. We have to work hard to keep our balance because the packs push us around. Our legs and thighs get sore quickly.

It is also getting hot; the midday sun is beating down on our backs. To our joy, we get a reward every time we pass one of the deep, dark crevices between the boulders: cool air floats from the crevices. Marcy crawls down into one, and it feels like being in an ice machine.

At last, we reach Summit Rock and the high point of the pass. I feel proud of Marcy. She has shown a lot of guts and strength to get up this trail. Now we can rest and admire the spectacular view of Wallface. An 1844 visitor described it as a "wild scene of terrible beauty."

We hear a *kack-kack-kack* and look up to see two birds soaring above the cliffs. They are the size of crows, but their light undersides and long, pointed wings tell us

▲ *Inset Above: Along the trail through Indian Pass. Marcy crawls into chilly caves.*

▶ *Right: At Summit Rock. We give our backs a rest as we admire the jagged cliffs of Wallface Mountain.*

The Adirondack Park has more than 2,000 miles of marked trails. Keeping these trails in shape is a lot of work. Branches and brush are cut back along the sides of the trail. Fallen trees are removed. Bridges are built. Stepping stones are put down, or wooden planks are used to create "boardwalks" across muddy areas. Rock steps or wooden ladders are installed in steep places to stop erosion.

Most of this work is done by hand, without the aid of power tools. And all of the wood, tools, and other supplies must be carried to the work area, which might be miles into the woods.

they are peregrine falcons. These birds are great skydivers, reaching speeds of up to 200 miles per hour. Falcons disappeared from the Adirondacks in the 1960s because of pesticide poisoning. Thanks to pollution controls and breeding programs, these amazing birds have returned.

We descend the other side of the pass. At some spots, we have to crawl on wooden ladders because the terrain is so steep. My legs ache, and sweat drips from my forehead. I look for my red bandanna but can't find it. I ask Marcy whether she knows where it is, and she says, "Mom, it's on your head."

At six o'clock we finally reach Wallface

◀ *Climbing down ladders in Indian Pass. When carrying a backpack, you have to go down facing the ladder. I go down first and help Marcy's feet find the ladder rungs.*

◀ *Left: Wallface Lean-to beside Indian Pass Brook*

▼ *Below: Preparing to cook on our single-burner stove. A small, red canister of white gas fuels the cookstove.*

Lean-to. It sits beside a brook, surrounded by yellow birch trees. What a magical place. Best of all, it is empty. The place belongs to the two of us.

Marcy filters water while I start making tea and hot cocoa. Then I boil water to add to our package of dehydrated food. Tonight's dinner is pad Thai (spicy noodles with vegetables and a peanut sauce).

After dinner, we have a special treat — backpacker's ice cream. It looks like a white, brown, or pink cube of chalk. When you put it in your mouth, your saliva mixes with the powder and turns into a goop that sort of reminds you of ice cream. Marcy eats the chocolate one, I eat the strawberry one, and we share the vanilla. It doesn't taste great, but I suppose it is better than eating boiled bark like the Algonquins!

As the woods grow dark, Marcy spreads our sleeping bags on the wooden floor. I wonder whether she is thinking about the bears, bats, and other creatures that might be in the woods. It doesn't matter; we are too tired to worry.

We lie side by side and close our eyes. The brook lulls us to sleep.

GHOST TOWN

Day 3, Friday, August 1

THERE IS LIGHT RAIN THIS MORNING AS WE BEGIN walking. An hour later, we reach a dirt road. Just a few yards down the road, we find shabby gray houses with broken windows, leaky roofs, rotted floors, and rusty hinges. This is a ghost town!

Just like in an old Western movie, it comes with a dusty street and tumbleweeds. It even has a spooky name: Deserted Village.

This is what remains of the grand ironworks started after Henderson's discovery of the ore bed. During the 1840s and early 1850s, this was a busy place. There were about thirty buildings, including a sawmill, a piggery, a bank, and even a schoolhouse. But it was difficult running the business from this remote spot. One day in 1857, the business closed and the workers left. It is said they just walked off, leaving tools and machines and furniture as they were. And there the buildings stayed. Deserted. Silent.

Sportsmen took over the run-down property for a while, but eventually they abandoned the spot, too. Now Mother Nature is reclaiming what is hers, pushing plants up through roads, porches, and old yards.

After lunch, Marcy and I leave the ghosts and hike toward Calamity Pond. We trudge along a logging road lined by tall stalks of grass. Butterflies flit along the trail and brighten our spirits. A few even join our procession. Grasshoppers want to come, too. One hitches a ride on Marcy's pack.

When we arrive at the shore of the pond, we spot a huge chunk of granite with David Henderson's name on it. The monument seems a strange sight in the woods, and a strange story goes with it.

Henderson came here looking for a source of waterpower for the iron forge. When his party arrived at the pond, Henderson saw some ducks and thought they would make a tasty dinner. He said to a guide, "You take my pistol and kill some of those ducks."

Something spooked the birds, and they flew away.

▲ *Above:* The Deserted Village of Adirondack *by Theodore R. Davis,* *from* Harper's Weekly, *November 21, 1868*

◀ *Opposite: Ghost town*

◀ *Opposite Inset: Exploring MacNaughton Cottage. We walk across the floorboards in the footsteps of Theodore Roosevelt. He was vice president when he stayed here in 1901. During the evening of Friday, September 13, he received a message: "The President is dying." Roosevelt raced by buggy to the nearest train station. Upon his arrival, he was told that McKinley had died. Roosevelt had become president of the United States.*

The lean-to has been a favorite woods shelter in the Adirondacks since the early 1800s. The sides were built of small trees or branches, with the front side left open to the campfire. Bark was laid across the top for a roof, and the dirt floor was covered with balsam branches to create a soft, good-smelling mattress. A skilled woodsman could make a lean-to in three-quarters of an hour, but it rarely remained standing more than a few months.

Today, permanent lean-tos have been built at popular camping spots. They are made of logs, and the floor is usually covered with boards. The three-sided hut, with its open front, makes you feel like a rugged mountaineer. While keeping you comfortable and dry, it lets you enjoy the sensation of sleeping in the woods: feeling the cool air, hearing the animal sounds, and tasting the morning mist.

THE SHANTY

The guide handed back the pistol and Henderson put it in his pack. A few moments later, Henderson put down his pack, and the gun struck a rock and fired. The shot hit Henderson.

Everyone wondered what had happened. Then Henderson whispered to the guide, "You must have left the pistol cocked." Within a few moments, Henderson passed away. It took the entire next day to carry his body out along the rough trail to the village.

Ever since, the pond has been called Calamity Pond, the stream Calamity Brook, and the nearby hill Calamity Mountain.

We move along the muddy trail and arrive at Calamity Lean-to #2 just ten minutes before the rain starts. How wonderful to have a roof over our heads! We drop our packs, unroll our sleeping bags, and take a nap. When we open our eyes, the rain has stopped. It is time to explore our new surroundings.

▶ Right: Outhouse with birch handle. At camping areas, there is usually an outhouse placed over a hole in the ground. When there is no outhouse, campers find a spot behind a tree.

◀ Opposite: The Shanty by Theodore R. Davis, from Harper's Weekly, November 21, 1868. Camping in a three-sided shanty, or "lean-to," is an Adirondack tradition.

First, I head to the outhouse. I marvel at the large, sleek birch door handle that has replaced the usual rusty metal one. Someone must have been pretty bored out here to do all that woodcarving.

Then I join Marcy down at the shore of Flowed Land. As its name suggests, this lake doesn't really belong here; it is flooded land created by a dam. Parts of the dam are broken, but for now, the man-made dam has been allowed to remain in the wilderness area.

We watch leeches wriggle through the water. Then loud splashes draw our attention to a stuck duck. It flaps its wings and splashes but goes nowhere. It must be caught on an underwater log or fishing line or something. Marcy wants to go set it free, but how can we? It is far out in the water, and it is a scared animal. It would probably peck me if I came near.

We decide to let nature take its course. The duck will either break free and fly away or it will become food for an otter or eagle. That is the way things happen out here.

As the sun sets, we put our food away carefully. There have been problems with bears in this area. To keep food safe, hikers used to put it in a bag and hang the bag from a rope strung between two trees. But bears are so smart they learned how to pull down the rope, bringing a bag of dinner with it.

I camped nearby last year and heard bears around my tent. They knocked down trees to get people's food. Bears seem to love peanut butter, but even the smell of toothpaste appeals to them. There is a notebook in the lean-to, and

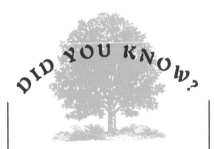
Black bears have always roamed the Adirondacks. But whereas other symbols of the wild have decreased in population, bears have multiplied. Since fewer hunters are shooting bears in the Adirondacks, their population has increased from about one thousand in the early 1900s to around five thousand today.

Bears usually weigh between 160 and 320 pounds, but they can get as large as 750 pounds. They enjoy eating wild berries, insects, nuts, and grasses. But experts say they will eat anything from honey to road kill.

▶ *A black bear*

someone wrote that one bear said, "I like Jell-O."

Our food should be safe in the canister. The bears can kick it around, but they cannot open it. Of course I don't really expect to see a bear. It is exciting to know these wild animals are out here — that is part of what makes going into the wilderness such an adventure — but rarely do you come face to face with one. Nor do you want to — they are wild and unpredictable.

To my surprise, a bear arrives at eight in the evening. It is huge, and it squats down right behind our lean-to. It looks as though the bear plans to stay awhile.

Marcy is thrilled but a little scared. This is her first encounter with a wild bear. It is so close that we can smell the rotten odor of wet fur. Its bright eyes glare at us, and we stare back. All of a sudden it lets out a loud grunt, and we jump.

Eventually the bear gets up and walks away without even sniffing at our food canister. Maybe it could tell we did not have any Jell-O.

Up Herbert Brook

Day 4, Saturday, August 2

"It's a great thing these days to leave civilization for a while and return to nature."

— Bob Marshall (1901–1939), hiker and conservationist

▲ *Following the streambed of Herbert Brook up the mountain*

TODAY WE ARE CLIMBING A MOUNTAIN. THE PEAK IS **4,360** FEET above sea level and our camp is 2,760 feet, so we will be going up 1,600 feet. That is not incredibly steep since it is spread over a few miles. However, there are two snags. First, there is no marked trail; we will have to bushwhack. Second, rain and thunderstorms are predicted.

Despite all that, Marcy and I want to go. It will be a chance to hike without our heavy packs, and it will be our first climb up this peak, named for a great Adirondacker. Mount Marshall honors the life of Bob Marshall, one of the most important conservationists of the twentieth century. He worked for the United States Forest Service and fought to protect America's wild lands.

Marshall hiked throughout the Rocky Mountains and Alaska, but his appreciation for wilderness started in the Adirondacks. In 1918, when he was seventeen, he decided to start climbing the tall mountains. His fourteen-year-old brother, George, came along, and so did forty-eight-year-old Herb Clark, who served as their guide.

Herb was an incredible mountain climber, especially when there was no trail to follow. He could sight a peak from a distant point, then walk for hours through the thick woods and emerge on the summit by the fastest and easiest route. At age fifty-one, he was still thought of as the fastest man in the pathless woods.

To keep the boys happy during their long walks, Herb loved to make up woods

Bob Marshall, Herb Clark, and George Marshall on the summit of Mount Marcy, about 1918

fables. He told one about a grandfather pickerel, which had gold teeth and spectacles, and another about Joe McGinnis, who had a disease that shrank him to the size of a baseball. The boys chuckled and walked, and soon they had climbed all the Adirondack peaks more than 4,000 feet tall — a total of forty-six peaks. No one had ever done that. They were the first "forty-sixers."

Others followed in the footsteps of Herb, Bob, and George, and eventually a club formed. The Adirondack Forty-Sixers now has more than five thousand members. The only requirement of membership is to climb all forty-six high peaks. (Recent measurements show that not all of the forty-six peaks are actually more than 4,000 feet tall, but the club has kept the original list of peaks anyway.)

I have been working toward this goal for fifteen years. This will be my forty-first high peak. I hope to reach forty-six before the end of the summer. Marcy might climb all the high peaks someday, too. She has already climbed twenty-four.

Today's hike is extra exciting because we are joining a group of hikers, and among them will be Robyn and Jonathan, great-grandchildren of guide Herb Clark. We plan to climb Mount Marshall by following Herbert Brook, which is named for Herb. It will feel as though he is guiding us, just as he guided Bob and George.

Despite the weather predictions, it is sunny as we begin our march into the woods and away from the hiking trail. Sometimes there is a deer path to follow. Sometimes we bushwhack through the trees. Most of the way, we follow Herbert Brook's streambed. It is a constant series of flumes and waterfalls tumbling over hard, smooth bedrock. Spongy moss and soft ferns line the banks.

Our shirts are wet with sweat and our lungs are gasping for air when we reach the summit. Yet we raise our arms and shout the hikers' cheer: "We made it!"

The very top is covered with trees, so we do just as Herb, Bob, and George did eighty-some years ago: we walk around and find ledges that jut out between the trees. The ledges offer surprisingly good views. From one, we look at the cliffs of Wallface, and from another we see a panorama of Flowed Land. We imagine the view

is just as it was years ago. "This is probably the wildest mountain in the Adirondacks," wrote Bob Marshall in 1922. "In it all there was not a sign to show that man had ever been there."

After lunch, we head down the trail. It has been a good day of climbing.

Our friends keep walking toward their cars, while we stay at our lean-to and cook dinner. At eight o'clock we watch for the bear. There it is, right on schedule!

It looks at us and we look at it. Looks like the same bear, and it probably thinks we look like the same campers — only dirtier and stinkier. Five long minutes go by before it finally goes over the hill. Then we hear the *thud, thud* of heavy footsteps on the hiking trail. The bear comes walking down the trail, crosses the brook, and goes to visit other campers.

▲ *Our jolly group of hikers on Mount Marshall. Jonathan (standing, left) and Robyn (standing, center) are the great-grandchildren of guide Herb Clark.*

Marcy's Journal
Saturday, August 2

I didn't get much sleep. The bear came back three times during the night. He kept going to visit the campers across the brook, and they kept trying to chase him away.

They kept yelling, "Go away! Go away!" Finally, they got really mad and screamed at him, "You, BEAR, you! Don't you have anything better to do?"

Mom and I giggled.

SPLITTING THE CLOUDS

Day 5, Sunday, August 3

▲ *William Learned Marcy, the namesake of Mount Marcy. Marcy was governor of New York State from 1832 to 1838. Under President James Polk, he served as secretary of war from 1845 to 1849; and under President Franklin Pierce, he served as secretary of state from 1853 to 1857.*

WHILE EXPLORERS WERE DISCOVERING THE mighty rivers and grand mountains of the West, the Adirondack high peaks were still almost completely unknown. As late as the 1830s, scientists claimed that no Adirondack peak rose higher than 2,600 feet. Finally, on August 5, 1837, a party of twelve men (three geologists, a botanist, a businessman, an artist, a teenager, and five guides) climbed Mount Marcy. They proved this Adirondack mountain was more than 5,000 feet tall.

Within a month, others set out to climb the great peak. At last, the world was discovering Mount Marcy.

Women started climbing the peak in the 1850s. Some found it easy, while others found it troublesome to walk in their long skirts, petticoats, and corsets. One lady said it was so difficult that she would not climb again even if the Queen of Sheba were coming up the other side to meet her. Another became so mad that she grabbed a knife and cut 10 inches from the bottom of her dress, leaving the remnants wrapped around a rock.

These ladies inspire Marcy and me. We decide to honor them by wearing long skirts during our hike over Mount Marcy.

A stretch of steep climbing lies ahead — a rise of more than 2,500 feet in elevation. This is when you learn about toughness. You just keep walking, lifting one leg after the other. Placing one footstep higher than the last, leaning on your walking stick, you push yourself up and over the next rock. There's nothing else to do but keep walking. As you walk, a strange thing happens: you fall into a rhythm, and the rhythm puts you into a sort of trance. You don't even feel yourself walking.

> *"Few fully understand what the Adirondack wilderness really is. It is a mystery even to those who have crossed and recrossed it."*
>
> — Verplanck Colvin (1847–1920)

◀ *Left: Crossing the Opalescent River on a suspension bridge*

▶ *Right: Upstream from the bridge, a narrow gorge called The Flume. The bed of the stream is filled with pebbles and boulders of opalescent feldspar. The rocks sparkle blue and green and gold in the sunlight.*

Your muscles don't hurt. You forget about your heavy pack. You forget about people and TV and power lines and shopping malls. The world is about tangled tree branches, moss carpets, rock cliffs, and water.

We hike along the edge of the green-tinted Opalescent River until it meets Feldspar Brook. Sometimes I lead; sometimes Marcy leads. The higher we climb, the fewer deciduous trees and the more balsam and spruce we see. The trees become short and tattered as we climb above 4,000 feet. We are now in the alpine zone.

Finally, Lake Tear of the Clouds emerges through the trees. It is a tiny pond — really just a bog — with sphagnum moss covering half the surface. It is hard to believe that this is the highest pond source of the Hudson River, but it is true. This is where the mighty river of the north begins its journey. From the summit of Mount Marcy 1,000 feet above, the waters drip down, collect in Lake Tear, and then flow down the Feldspar and the Opalescent to the Hudson, past Albany and Manhattan, more than 200 miles to the Atlantic Ocean.

At the pond's edge, we stop to rest. I give Marcy some pepperoni sticks, and they seem to revive her. When we resume our walking, she takes one of my hiking

29

DID YOU KNOW?

Verplanck Colvin spent more than thirty years exploring and measuring the Adirondack peaks. He started his explorations in 1865, and by 1872 he had convinced state officials to appoint him chief of the Adirondack Survey. He worked in rain and snow, hauling heavy equipment to the summits, building signal stations, and taking measurements.

Every year in his reports to the state, he described his difficult tasks and his amazing discoveries. He also pushed for the protection of the Adirondacks and played an important role in the creation of the Adirondack Forest Preserve. He insisted the forests were the "watershed" of New York, providing a flow of water to the middle and lower portions of the state.

▼ *Lake Tear as Colvin saw it in 1872. He called it "a minute, unpretending tear of the clouds — as it were — a lonely pool, shivering in the breezes of the mountains."*

▶ *Opposite: On the summit of Mount Marcy, watching a game of hide-and-go-seek between the clouds and mountaintops. In the mid-1800s, the grand scene made a climber remark, "By golly, there's nothing but mountains, and where they couldn't get in a big one they sharpened up a little one and stuck it in."*

poles. It helps her on the steep section, and she seems to find a hidden source of energy.

Giant, dark clouds follow us up the rocky face. We fear that as soon as we reach the top we will have to run down the other side to escape the storm. Or maybe Mount Marcy will live up to its nickname, Tahawus, which means "Cloud Splitter."

This is why I gave my daughter the name Marcy. I hoped that she would split the clouds of darkness and sorrow. I hoped that she would always reach for the high ground, the truth, the top of the mountain. She is struggling to reach the top today, but I think she will make it.

At last the dark clouds separate and move away from the mountain maidens. Yet the view is spoiled by patches of fog drifting in and out.

I start to complain about the storm and the haze. Then suddenly I realize that despite everything, there is no place I would rather be than right where I am, on top of Cloud Splitter with my Marcy.

Hand in hand, we step onto the summit.

We are at the highest point in New York: 5,344 feet. We stand on the boundary between sky and earth. We look down over all the other mountaintops. We yell as loudly as we can, but our voices do not echo because there is nothing to rebound the sound; we are above the mountain walls.

At our feet is very old rock, more than one billion years old. It is called anorthosite, the same type of rock as that found on the moon.

It appears that the entire summit is bare rock. When we look closer, we see thousands of small plants. These kinds of plants have been growing here since before the last ice sheets swept through the region about thirteen thousand years ago. They are common in Alaska, Newfoundland, and the Arctic but are rarely found this far south. They grow only at the tops of the very highest Adirondack mountains.

In the late 1960s, scientist Edwin Ketchledge found that hikers were trampling the rare plants and causing soil erosion. This fragile layer of soil and dead peat took thousands of years to accumulate — yet hiking boots can destroy it in a few minutes.

That's when Ketchledge found a way to restore the alpine vegetation. First, he planted common grass, which stopped the soil erosion. Native species of moss, liverwort, and lichen began to grow. Then alpine plants, such as mountain sandwort, three-toothed cinquefoil, and dwarf birch, started growing again, too.

Today there are short rock walls to show hikers where they should walk. Marcy and I are careful to stay on the trail. We want to protect the fragile habitat.

Other hikers watch us as we stroll around the summit. It is fun to swirl our long skirts and let the wind poof them into parachutes. It reminds me of the poem Marcy wrote after her first time on top of this mountain.

DID YOU KNOW?

The rock mass underlying the High Peaks region is anorthosite. It is an unusual rock, made mostly of feldspar. It is similar to the rock that makes up the bright areas of the moon. The mass of anorthosite under Mount Marcy occupies more than 3,300 square miles and is the largest single anorthosite body in the United States.

31

MOUNT MARCY

The wind lifts my soul.

My soul lifts my spirit and
makes me rise too.

I fly with the falcon.

I zoom through the water
with the otter and beaver.

I fly again.

I fly over many mountains.

I land and zoom back down
on the wings I have.

Down to the valley.

— Marcy Weber, July 2000

DID YOU KNOW?

In the Adirondacks, the areas above 4,000 feet are considered the alpine zone. At this elevation, the soil becomes shallow, and a thick layer of peat covers the bedrock. The temperatures are cold, the wind is strong, and the snowfall is heavy. Not many plants can survive in those conditions.

Balsam fir and black spruce do grow here, but even they are only a few feet tall, with tangled branches. They are called krummholz, meaning "crooked woods."

Above 4,900 feet is the home of tundra vegetation. It is a rare habitat and one of the things that make the Adirondacks so special. There are only about 85 acres of alpine tundra in New York, scattered across the tops of twenty high peaks. These isolated ecosystems are sometimes thought of as "islands in the sky."

The dark clouds return, and we decide to head down. It might seem strange, but the down part is as difficult as the up. We slip and slide and sink into mudholes. Our knees ache from pounding down the rocks. Our feet scream for us to stop, but we have no choice. We climbed into the clouds; now we have to come down.

Marcy falls a few times but always stands up and continues. She doesn't even complain or ask for a rest.

We make it about halfway before we feel raindrops on our heads. I guess we are going to get wet. Five minutes later, the sun comes out and we are hot and sweaty. Mountain weather is unpredictable, and we have learned to accept its moods.

Marcy isn't talking much. I imagine she is thinking about birds and frogs and trees and soft beds and food that doesn't come from a plastic package.

We arrive at Johns Brook Lodge just in time for dinner — meatloaf, roasted vegetables, and mashed potatoes.

The lodge is like an oasis in the forest welcoming wet, tired, hungry hikers. It is 3½ miles from the closest road. All lodge supplies have to be dropped by helicopter or carried in on the backs of "hut boys." Of course, some of the "boys" who work at the lodge are really girls.

It is a very rustic place. There are no power lines or telephone lines. But there is an indoor bathroom! It has a sink and soap and hot water heated by propane gas.

We scrub our arms and legs and faces until they tingle. Then we look in the mirror to admire our cleanliness. Instead we see messy strands of frizzy hair. We forgot we haven't used a comb in five days.

BUNKROOM LUXURY

Day 6, Monday, August 4

EVEN THOUGH THERE WERE TEN PEOPLE IN THE BUNKROOM LAST NIGHT, I HAD A wonderful sleep. Oh, the luxury of a soft mattress and a fluffy pillow!

My head and limbs feel pampered, but my stomach still feels skinny. So I eat three plates of pancakes. Marcy eats a dozen slices of bacon.

Yesterday was tough. So were the four previous days. We need a day of rest, and this is a perfect resting day. It is cloudy, breezy, and cool. More rain showers are likely.

We clean our boots, eat snacks, nap together in Marcy's bunk, and eat more snacks. Later, Marcy spends an hour floating driftwood down the brook while I soak my feet in the cool water.

I wish this trip would never end. I like living on the trail. I like not knowing what might come our way, and I like the slow pace. I am enjoying the little moments, such as watching a tiny toad hop across the trail or letting a caterpillar crawl up my arm.

In late afternoon, it pours rain; then the thunder and lightning start. Marcy sings, "Hallelujah!" She is glad to be inside.

After dinner, Marcy plays card games with two girls, but by 8:30 she is ready for bed. She asks whether we can end the trip early. I say, "We'll see what happens."

I hope she has more energy in the morning. I don't want to cut the trip short. Of course, another day of rain might change my mind.

▼ *Sharing a laugh in Johns Brook Lodge. Even though the bunkroom is crowded and smelly, we appreciate its warmth and dryness.*

Down in the Valley

Day 7, Tuesday, August 5

> "A howling wilderness does not howl: it is the imagination of the traveller that does the howling."

— Henry David Thoreau, nature writer, *The Maine Woods*, 1864

▲ *Above: Taking a dip in Johns Brook*

▶ *Above Right: Running along the trail to the Garden*

BEFORE BREAKFAST, I WALK TO THE BROOK AND WATCH A DEER FEEDING ON A BUSH. Or is she watching me?

This is wilderness: when you blend with the natural world; sit and watch the mist rise from the valley; listen to the brook gurgling over the rocks; inhale the mountain air.

After breakfast, I go swimming at a water hole with Marcy and her friends. Then we pack. Since rain is expected, I consider changing our plans. I propose taking a shorter route out of the valley and then driving to Adirondak Loj. Marcy shouts, "Yes!" So that is what we do.

The strange spelling of lodge as "Loj" and Adirondak without a "c" is the legacy of Melvil Dewey. Besides creating the Dewey Decimal Classification system for libraries, Dewey promoted simplified spelling. He thought it was a waste of time to write unnecessary letters. So, since he helped build the place, it was called Adirondak Loj.

That was way back in 1927. When the new owners, the Adirondack Mountain Club, took over in 1959, they kept the odd spelling.

As soon as we arrive at the Loj, we run to the shower. It has been six days since we washed our hair, and it takes a big glob of shampoo to clean out the grubby strands.

Marcy decides to go kayaking on Heart Lake. She has never been in a kayak before, but she is not afraid. She jumps right in and zooms across the lake. A loon dives under the water in front of her.

The common loon, or "great northern diver," is one of my favorite animals. It has a beautiful voice — a sort of ghostly laugh. To me, it is the call of the wild.

When Marcy comes to shore, we explore the lakeside. Near a big stump, we find crumbling bricks and pieces of broken china. These are the remains of a grand hotel called Adirondack Lodge. An inventor named Henry Van Hoevenberg built it in 1878.

"Mr. Van" (as his friends called him) liked to hike in the woods and wanted to show other people how to enjoy the woods, too. Artists, authors, philosophers, and particularly people with ill health wanted to escape the crowded, dirty, noisy cities. Places like Adirondack Lodge made "roughing it" comfortable; people could get into the woods yet still have the luxury of a hotel.

Unfortunately, Mr. Van went bankrupt and had to sell the lodge. A few years later, his friend Melvil Dewey bought the property. Then another tragedy struck. Fires burned throughout the Adirondacks in the spring of 1903, and on June 3 strong winds pushed fires toward the lodge. Nothing could be done to stop the

▲ *Henry Van Hoevenberg was sometimes called the Man of Leather because he wore leather suits in the woods. Leather lasted much longer than corduroy cloth, he said.*

▲ *Above Inset: Adirondack Lodge, burned in 1903. The lodge was built with six hundred straight and tall spruce trees. It was claimed to be the largest log building in the world at the time.*

▶ *Right: Relaxing in the living room of Adirondak Loj, built in 1927*

Kayaking on Heart Lake. It is Marcy's first time in a kayak, but she is a whiz with the paddle.

DID YOU KNOW?

The Adirondack Mountain Club (ADK) is a club for people interested in hiking, canoeing, skiing, and camping. ADK also promotes conservation of natural resources, environmental education, and the protection of the New York State Forest Preserve. Members do trail work, attend workshops, go on outings, and share advice.

ADK has about thirty-five thousand members. The club owns and runs Johns Brook Lodge near Keene Valley, as well as Adirondak Loj, the High Peaks Information Center, and the Loj campground near Lake Placid.

flames. The grand lodge burned to the ground.

In 1927 a smaller lodge, the current "Loj," was built several yards to the north. When the Adirondack Mountain Club bought it, they enlarged the structure. It now has beds for forty-six people and a great kitchen. We devour a pasta dinner and strawberry shortcake.

At 9:30, we hear the crash of thunder and see streaks of lightning. Soon it is pouring rain. That makes five days of rain.

LANDSLIDE

Day 8, Wednesday, August 6

▲ *Landslide on Mount Colden near Avalanche Pass, which occurred in 1999. At the base of the Colden slide, 200 feet of trail were buried beneath tons of rock, soil, and trees. It took trail crews five days of cutting to make a path through the jumbled mass. Landslides are common in this area because of thin soil and steep mountainsides.*

IT IS TOO FINE A DAY TO SIT STILL. MARCY AND I DECIDE TO TAKE A DAY HIKE to Avalanche Pass. She laughs and runs and jumps in the mud. Then she trips over a root and falls flat on her face. She is not hurt, but she slows down a little.

We arrive at a landslide on the western face of Mount Colden. There are many old slides here — that is why it is called Avalanche Pass — but this is a new slide. It was created in 1999 by Hurricane Floyd. Drenching rains loosened the thin soil from the rocks, and then suddenly it all let go. The trees and dirt came sliding down the steep mountainside. Now there is a long stretch of open rock, and at the bottom trees lie in heaps like giant pick-up sticks. It is another reminder that wilderness is not neat and tidy like a front lawn; it can be ugly and rotten and troublesome.

Our first hurdle is getting over the mass of mangled trees and dirt and rocks. When we finally reach the open slide, the second hurdle appears. Marcy is scared to climb up the bare rock.

I give her time to think and work out a solution. Slowly, she drops to her knees and crawls out onto the rock. Inch by inch she gathers courage. Finally, she stands up and discovers that the surface is not slippery like glass; instead it grips like sandpaper. I follow her and find it's fun to walk through the openness.

Marcy's Journal
Wednesday, August 6

I was scared today. I did not want to climb that slide. But Mom had so much faith in me. She believed I could do it. So I kept going, and I am glad I did.

There was nothing to be afraid of. It was awesome up there on that open rock. I felt so proud of myself.

We sit next to each other on the wide slab of rock and eat turkey sandwiches and chewy chocolate chip–banana brownies. The views are beautiful, but the real joy is just sitting together, in the open, not speaking, just soaking in the peace and quiet. We feel like the only two people in the world.

On the way back to the Loj, rain pours down on us, but we don't put on raincoats — we enjoy nature's shower. Marcy can't believe I am letting her get soaked.

Mud and Guts

Day 9, Thursday, August 7

THIS MORNING WE DRIVE TO A LAUNDROMAT AND WASH TWO LOADS OF muddy socks and stinky shirts.

We stuff the clean clothes into our packs and prepare for four days in the woods. Once again, the weather forecast includes a good chance of rain every day, and the possibility of thunderstorms.

It is 3:30 when we pull the car into the parking lot at Deserted Village. I expect a flat and easy walk to the big pond, named Duck Hole. I think we can make the 7-mile hike in less than three hours.

Wrong! The trail goes up and down little hills. It is hard to find good footing because the week of rain has turned every rock and root into a slippery slide. Even the flat stretches are tricky. They hold puddles and thick mud — and big green frogs. In some places, bridges are missing and we have to cross streams on logs and rocks.

Just when we think we have reached dry ground, we find ourselves at a beaver pond. There is no sign of the beaver; it has probably moved to a new home. But it has left behind a dam and

▲ *Above: Crossing a beaver dam. Keeping my balance is not easy.*

◀ *Left: Frog trying to hide in a puddle*

41

Marcy's Journal
Thursday, August 7

 This has definitely been the worst day: 7 miles in four hours. It was the worst trail I've ever been on.

 We had to pitch the tent on rocky ground, and we bent all the stakes. Things kept getting worse. We had to eat this horrible macaroni and cheese. Then it rained, so the tent got soaked. It was a horrible day. I hope things go better tomorrow.

flooded woodland. The only path across is on top of the dam, so we step onto the mish-mash of mud and sticks. Our boots squish in the mud and slip on the wet sticks. It requires a tricky balancing act to keep from sliding into the pond.

It is a tough hike, but at least the terrain is beautiful. Jagged cliffs rise above our heads. Emerald green moss, pea-green ferns, and loads of mushrooms cover the ground.

The approaching darkness keeps us moving as fast as we can. Finally, we arrive at Duck Hole. Both lean-tos are occupied, so we pitch our tent in a meadow right beside blue gentians and red raspberry bushes. We cook dinner quickly and then crawl into our sleeping bags. It is a sweet home for two tired girls.

DID YOU KNOW?

The beaver is the largest rodent in the Adirondacks. It can be as much as 4 feet long, weigh 60 pounds, and chop full-grown trees with its powerful front teeth. Then the skillful beaver can put the trees together to build a dam and create a pond.

In pre-Colonial times, there may have been more than a million Adirondack beavers. Because their fur was ideal for making fur-felt hats, popular in Europe, they were trapped in great numbers. By 1895, the Adirondack beaver population was fewer than ten. Trapping was halted. Within twenty years, beavers had been restored and trapping was allowed again. Today, the population of Adirondack beavers is estimated to be about 30,000.

▲ *Above: Salamander (also called a red eft) exploring the wet forest*

▶ *Opposite: A tree trying to reach its roots to the ground. Somehow this tree manages to make its home atop two boulders.*

▶ *Opposite Inset: A burl (big, round bump) on a tree. This bump happens when a twig bud fails to grow normally. Although it looks weird, a burl usually does not harm a tree.*

AT DUCK HOLE

Day 10, Friday, August 8

IN THE MORNING WE FIND THAT THE OTHER CAMPERS have left, so we move our stuff to Duck Hole Lean-to #2. We pitch the tent so that it will dry in the sunshine.

This spot feels remote and wild. The wind howls in the distance, and there are ragged mountain peaks. Lily pads float on the surface of the pond, and hemlocks and pines line the shore. There is plenty of company, too. Chickadees, butterflies, grasshoppers, loons, woodpeckers, and ducks roam Duck Hole.

Even the outhouse is extraordinary. The sign on the door says NAT WELL'S PARLOR OF MUSE. It is a strange place to sit and ponder your dreams, but the view is quite pretty. Through the open doorway, I can peek at the forest, the hills, and the ripples on the pond.

To our surprise, it is a warm, sunny day. To think I almost canceled this part of the trip! And now this is the best weather yet.

We have not seen another person for hours. We have the entire world to ourselves. I go swimming in the deep pool in front of the log dam. It is wonderful to lie back and float in the water like a lily pad.

▲ Above: Fixing noodles for dinner. The smoky campfire keeps the mosquitoes away.

▶ Opposite Top Left: A refreshing swim in Duck Hole

▶ Opposite Top Right: Resting in our tent

Marcy is a grasshopper in the meadow. Her long legs pounce through prickly berry bushes, with her long hair chasing behind. After her walk, she settles into the tent to read Tolkien's *The Lord of the Rings: Part Two: The Two Towers*. I didn't want to bring the book; it was extra weight. But I decided to let her have this luxury. Besides, I recalled that book pages do have practical uses. In an emergency, they can be used as fire starters, or as toilet paper.

In the afternoon, we decide to build a campfire. It is legal to have fires in this area of the Adirondacks. I search for dry sticks, but everything is wet from yesterday's

rain. Marcy gathers birch bark to help kindle the damp wood. Working together, we manage to get a fire started.

Later, while I am fanning the flames, a huge garter snake crawls toward the fire. I scream and run away. Marcy grabs a stick, picks up the snake, and carries it into the meadow.

I come out of hiding and start to cook dinner. Just then, big booms of thunder echo off the mountains. We manage to heat our noodles before the raindrops arrive. For two hours, the thunder and lightning circle above our heads and the rain pours down. We listen to the *drip, piddle, splat* of water dropping from the lean-to's roof into the moat that has formed around us.

As the sky finally brightens, three loons swim near our camp and announce their presence with wild calls.

After the sun sinks behind the hills, we light a candle. Its soft glow casts a brightness and warmth into the damp, dark woods. Somehow we seem to sense that this will be our last night of camping. Neither of us wants to go to sleep. We want to make this time together last as long as we can.

Marcy reads her book by candlelight while I lie beside her and listen to the silence. Finally we put out the candle and snuggle into our sleeping bags. Before I close my eyes, the moon peeks out of the clouds and shines on Duck Hole.

This is not a "dismal" wilderness. It is a bright and wondrous place, a place I do not want to leave.

THE PEAT BOG TRACK

The peat bog track
Goes on and on.
You wish your house were farther in.
The leaf and the log,
The bee and the toad,
Help to guide you on your way.
The mountains are white.
The air's growing cold,
And you just want to say,
Keep me — past streams and weeds.
Don't let me back,
I want to learn the ways of those
*   gone loose.*
I have been penned up,
For so many years.
My brothers and sisters kept me
*   back,*
Now I travel without fear or load.

— Marcy Weber

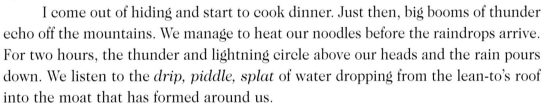

Marcy's Journal
Friday, August 8

I am surprised to find that there are carrots, pasta, and evaporated milk on the shelf in the lean-to. Obviously there are no bears around here.

I was lazy today. I read my book, built a fire, and swam. Then it rained. Everything happened in that order.

FAREWELL

Day 11, Saturday, August 9

As I drink my coffee, the ducks bathe and preen. The sun rises over MacNaughton Mountain and lifts the mist from the lake into the treetops, and then, like magic, the mist disappears.

Despite the serene setting, I know we must leave. The pond rose 4 inches last night, and more rain is on the way. The streams along the trail may become too high to cross, and we could be trapped in the woods. The wise choice is to head out today.

As we pack, Carl arrives in his canoe. Marcy hopes Carl will let her ride the canoe part of the way. She is not eager to retrace her steps over that horrible trail back to Deserted Village.

Carl agrees to let Marcy paddle across Duck Hole while he and I tote our packs along the hiking trail. Thunder roars in the distance, and I am glad we are on our way home.

Marcy meets us at the end of the lake, and Carl hoists the canoe onto his back. He looks like a turtle with a long yellow shell. When we reach the shore of Henderson Lake, Marcy steps into the boat again. I feel a little nervous as I wave good-bye. She has canoed many times, but always within my sight. I am uneasy about her going across this big lake. But I am also excited for her, because this is a wild and secluded place and she is getting a rare chance to explore it.

Marcy's Journal
Saturday, August 9

After Carl came, I went out in the canoe on Duck Hole. It was fun to see our lean-to from the pond. Paddling was much better than walking.

I met Mom and Carl at a little bay. Then I had to walk for a few miles.

I canoed again on Henderson Lake. After paddling for half an hour, I was in the middle of the lake. It was very quiet there. It rained a little, but I didn't mind because I had the whole place to myself.

I had never been to this lake before and almost forgot which way I needed to go to find the dock. I was glad when I found my way to it.

It takes us an hour to walk around the lake. When we arrive at the dock, Marcy is already waiting for us and wearing a big smile.

Deserted Village, and the end of the trail, is only a mile away. Marcy can feel the finish, and she lets all her energy loose. She hoots and hollers. She splashes in puddles and stomps through mudholes.

At the end of the trail, we compare dirty hair, scratched arms, and muddy boots. Marcy is the winner.

I feel like a winner, too, because she tells me, "I had the best time of my life."

Our journey is over. Or maybe a new one is beginning.

I glance over at the crumbling houses trying to survive amid the wild grass and hungry saplings. It is hard to believe that Deserted Village was once a thriving town, and before that it was an old-growth forest, and before that it was covered by a glacier. I realize that change is sure to happen. It is as unstoppable in nature as in Marcy and me. Just as nature's rhythms rise and fall, blend and separate, so do we.

Even as we dream new dreams and seek other adventures, we will always remember the days we shared as two in the wilderness.

▲ Above: Two in the Wilderness

◀ Opposite: Alone on Duck Hole. Marcy enjoys paddling the canoe and giving her legs a rest.

▼ Below: Loons

More on the Subject

BOOKS

Our Wilderness: How the People of New York Found, Changed and Preserved the Adirondacks by Michael Steinberg (Adirondack Mountain Club, 1995) is a history of the Adirondack Park. 100 pages. Ages 10 and up.

Kids on the Trail! by Rose Rivezzi and David Trithart (Adirondack Mountain Club, 1997) describes sixty-two hikes, treks, walks, strolls, and opportunities to explore and cavort with children on trails throughout the Adirondack Park. 175 pages. Ages 10 and up.

Adventures in Hiking: A Young Peoples' Guide to the Adirondacks by Barbara McMartin (North Country Books, 2001) teaches young people how to hike and where to hike in the Adirondacks. 110 pages. Ages 10 and up.

Adirondack Wildguide: A Natural History of the Adirondack Park by Michael G. DiNunzio (Adirondack Mountain Club, 2001) describes the plants and animals found in the various environments within the Adirondacks. 160 pages. Adult.

Adirondacks: Views of an American Wilderness by Carl E. Heilman II (Rizzoli International Publications, Inc., 1999) is a book of amazing photographs of wild places in the Adirondacks. 160 pages. Adult.

The Adirondack Reader: Third Edition, edited by Paul Jamieson and Neal Burdick (Adirondack Mountain Club, 2005), is a collection of writings about the Adirondack region. Adult.

WEB SITES

www.adkmuseum.org
Adirondack Museum

www.adkcurriculum.org
Adirondack Curriculum Project

www.adknature.org
Natural History Museum of the Adirondacks

www.dec.state.ny.us
New York State Department of Environmental Conservation

www.northnet.org/adirondackvic
Adirondack Park Visitor Interpretive Centers (operated by the New York State Adirondack Park Agency)

www.adirondacklife.com
Adirondack Life magazine

www.adk46r.org
Adirondack Forty-Sixers Club

www.adk.org
Adirondack Mountain Club

Index